A MUSICAL JOURNEY
EPISODES I–VI

MUSIC BY JOHN WILLIAMS
ARRANGED BY TOM GEROU

Produced by
Alfred Music Publishing Co., Inc.
P.O. Box 10003
Van Nuys, CA 91410-0003
alfred.com

Printed in USA.

No part of this book shall be reproduced, arranged, adapted, recorded, publicly performed, stored in a retrieval system, or transmitted by any means without written permission from the publisher. In order to comply with copyright laws, please apply for such written permission and/or license by contacting the publisher at alfred.com/permissions.

ISBN-10: 0-7390-6718-4
ISBN-13: 978-0-7390-6718-5

CONTENTS

EPISODES I–VI
    20th Century Fox Fanfare 8
    Star Wars (Main Title) 10

EPISODE I: THE PHANTOM MENACE
    Anakin's Theme 14
    Duel of the Fates 16

EPISODE II: ATTACK OF THE CLONES
    Across the Stars (Love Theme) 18

EPISODE III: REVENGE OF THE SITH
    Battle of the Heroes 22

EPISODE IV: A NEW HOPE
    Binary Sunset 24
    Cantina Band 26
    Jawa Sandcrawler 30
    Princess Leia's Theme 32
    The Throne Room 36

EPISODE V: THE EMPIRE STRIKES BACK
    The Imperial March (Darth Vader's Theme) 40
    May the Force Be with You 42
    Yoda's Theme 44

EPISODE VI: RETURN OF THE JEDI
    Luke and Leia 48

20ᵀᴴ CENTURY FOX FANFARE

Composed by **Alfred Newman**
Arranged by Tom Gerou

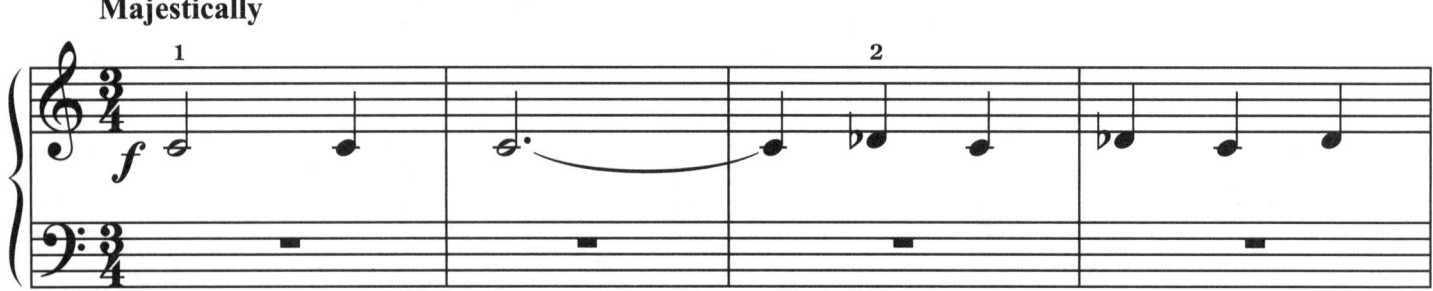

Optional Duet Accompaniment (Play solo part 1 octave higher than written.)

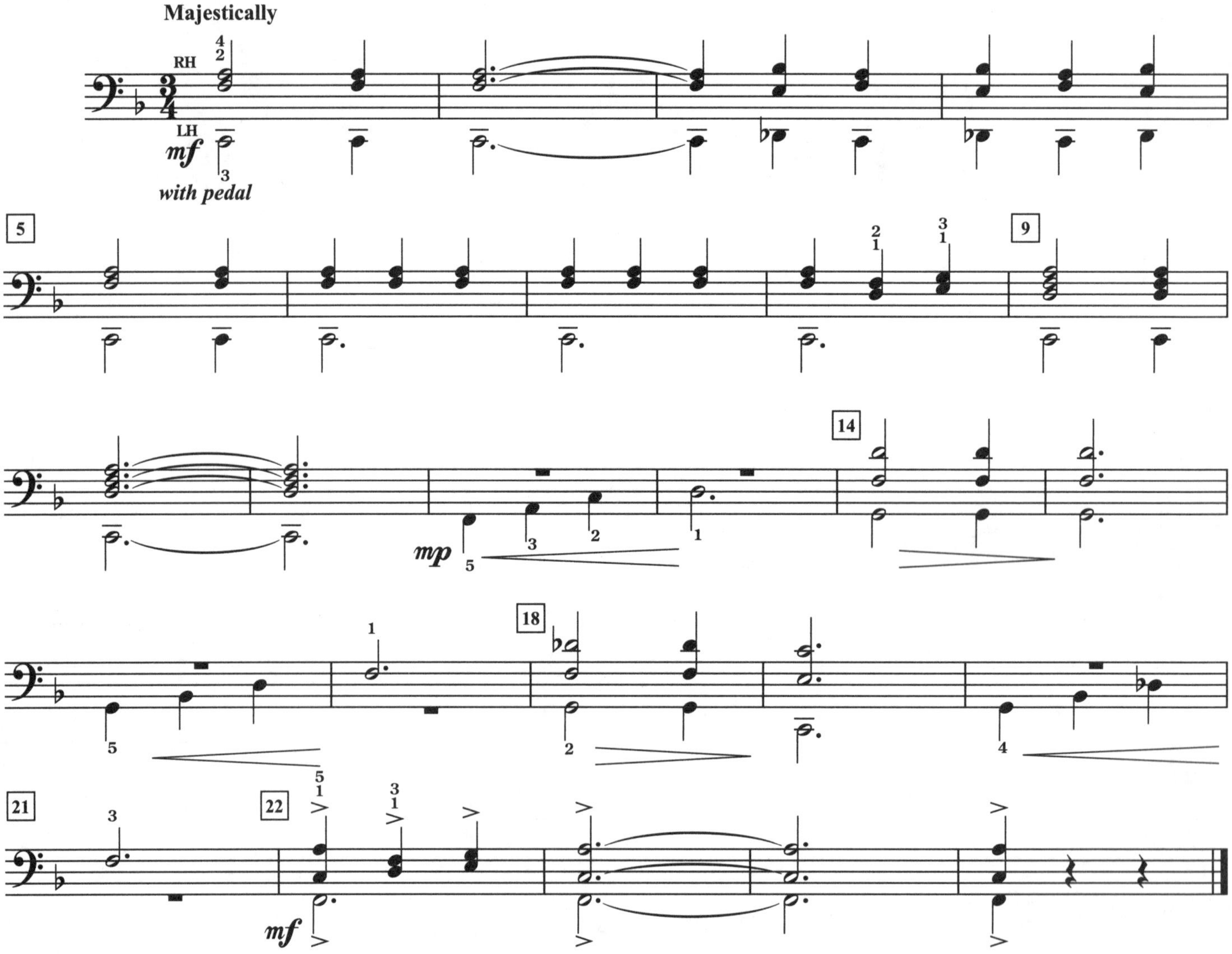

© 1956 (Renewed) TWENTIETH CENTURY MUSIC CORP.
Copyright Assigned 1996 to T C F MUSIC PUBLISHING, INC.
All Rights Reserved Used By Permission

STAR WARS
(Main Title)

Music by JOHN WILLIAMS
Arranged by Tom Gerou

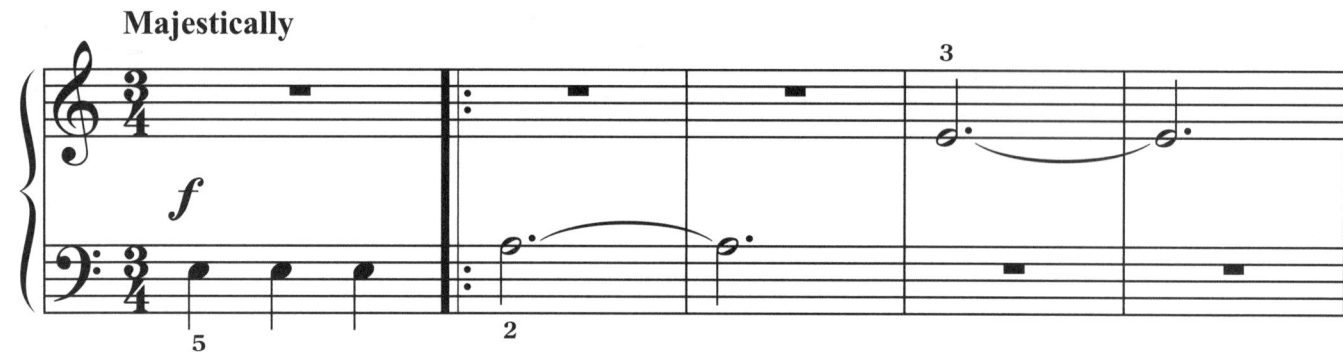

Optional Duet Accompaniment (Play solo part 1 octave higher than written.)

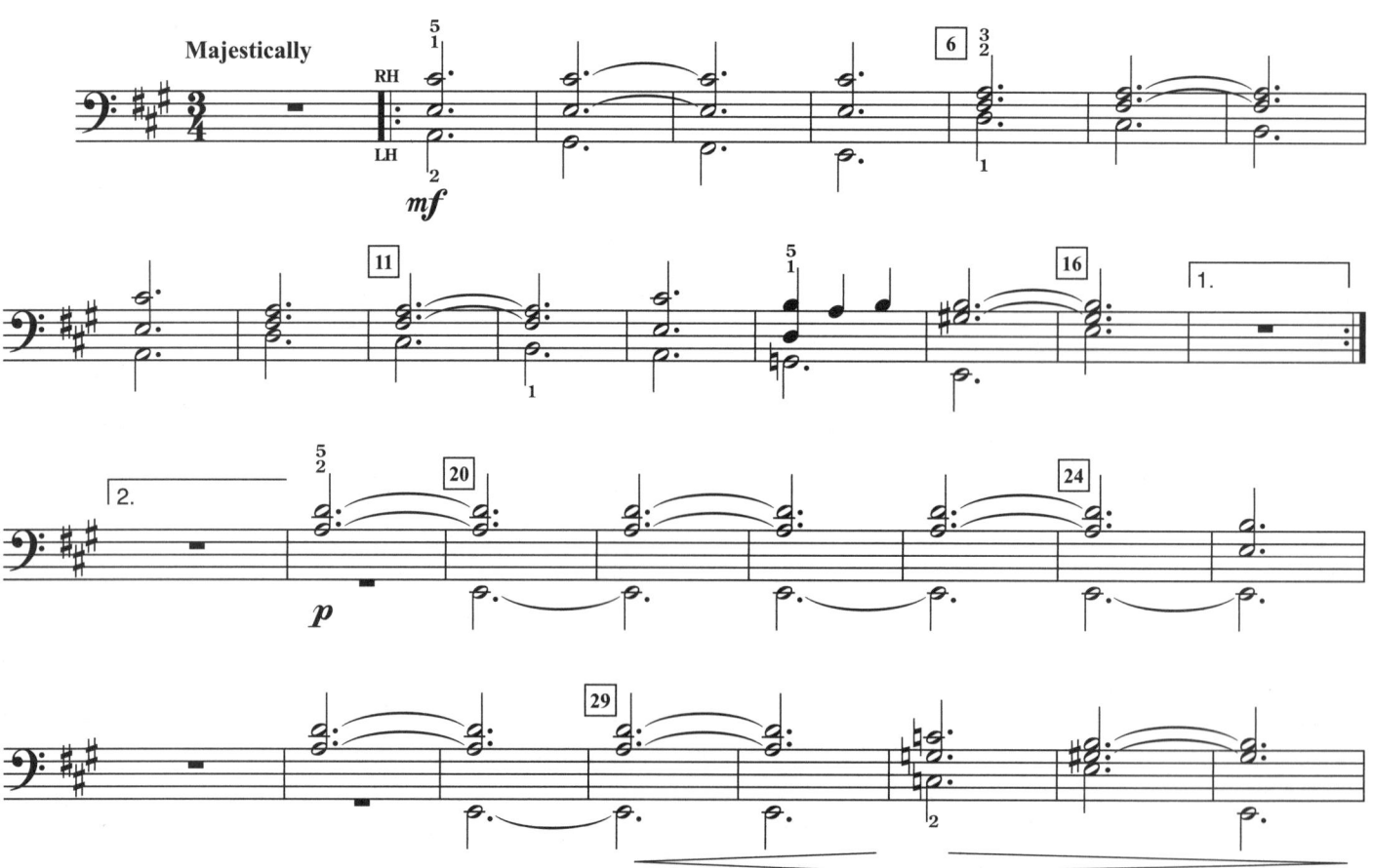

© 1977 (Renewed) WARNER-TAMERLANE PUBLISHING CORP. and BANTHA MUSIC
All Rights Administered by WARNER-TAMERLANE PUBLISHING CORP.
All Rights Reserved

ANAKIN'S THEME

Music by JOHN WILLIAMS
Arranged by Tom Gerou

Optional Duet Accompaniment (Play solo part 1 octave higher than written.)

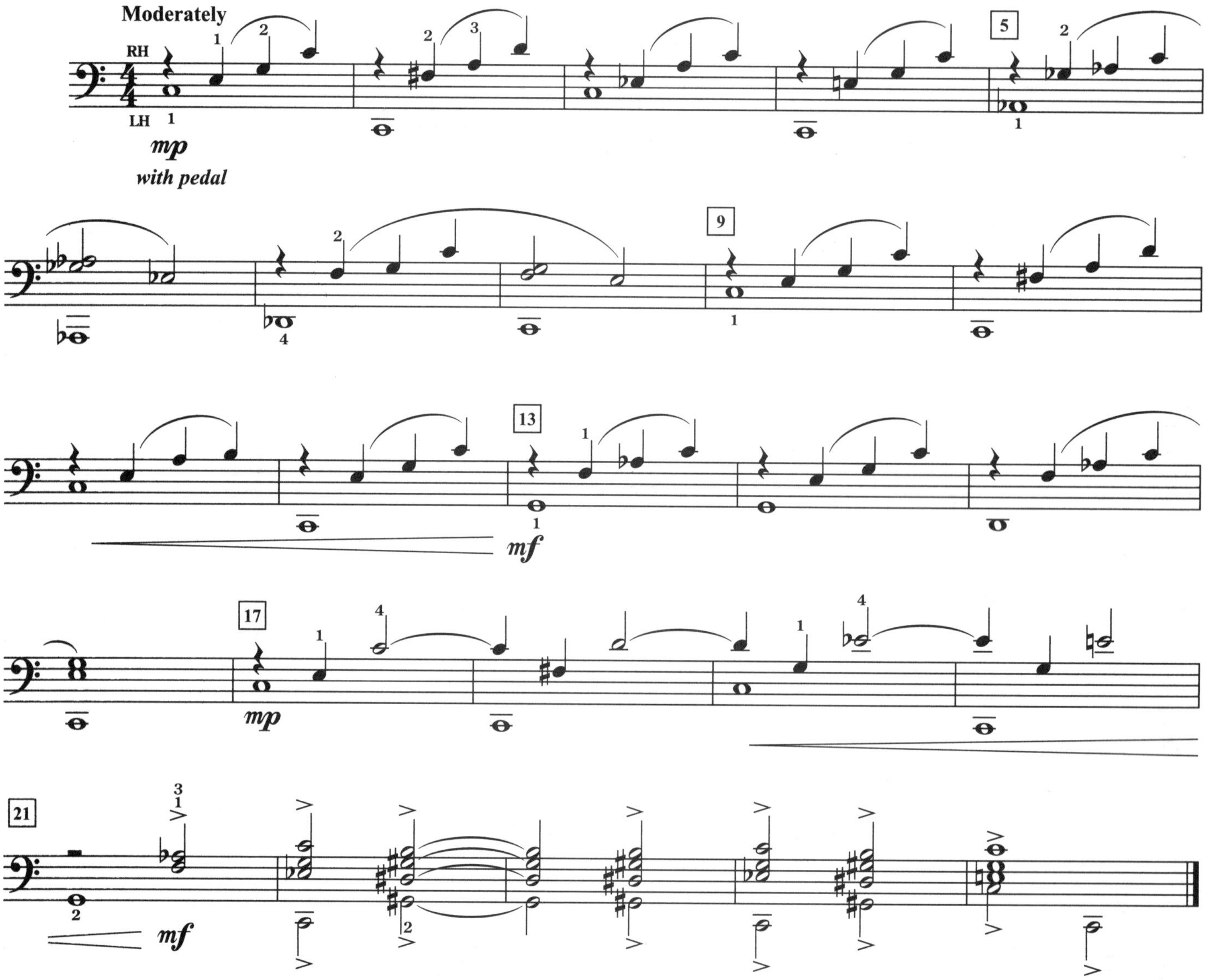

© 1999 BANTHA MUSIC
All Rights on behalf of BANTHA MUSIC Administered by WARNER-TAMERLANE PUBLISHING CORP.
All Rights Reserved

DUEL OF THE FATES

Music by JOHN WILLIAMS
Arranged by Tom Gerou

Fast, with great force

Optional Duet Accompaniment (Play solo part 1 octave higher than written.)

Fast, with great force

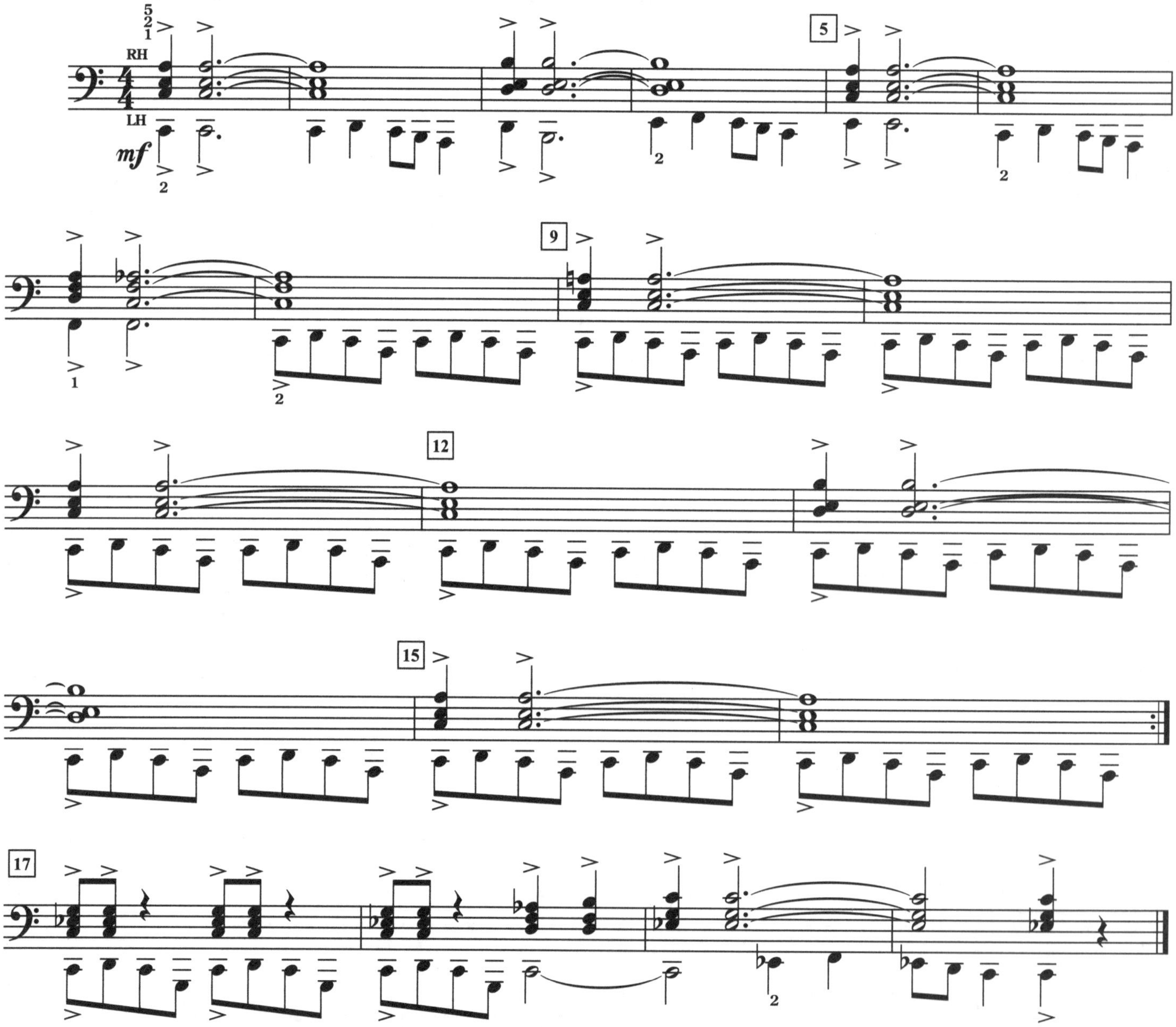

© 1999 BANTHA MUSIC
All Rights Administered by WARNER-TAMERLANE PUBLISHING CORP.
All Rights Reserved

ACROSS THE STARS
(Love Theme)

Music by **JOHN WILLIAMS**
Arranged by Tom Gerou

Optional Duet Accompaniment (Play solo part 1 octave higher than written.)

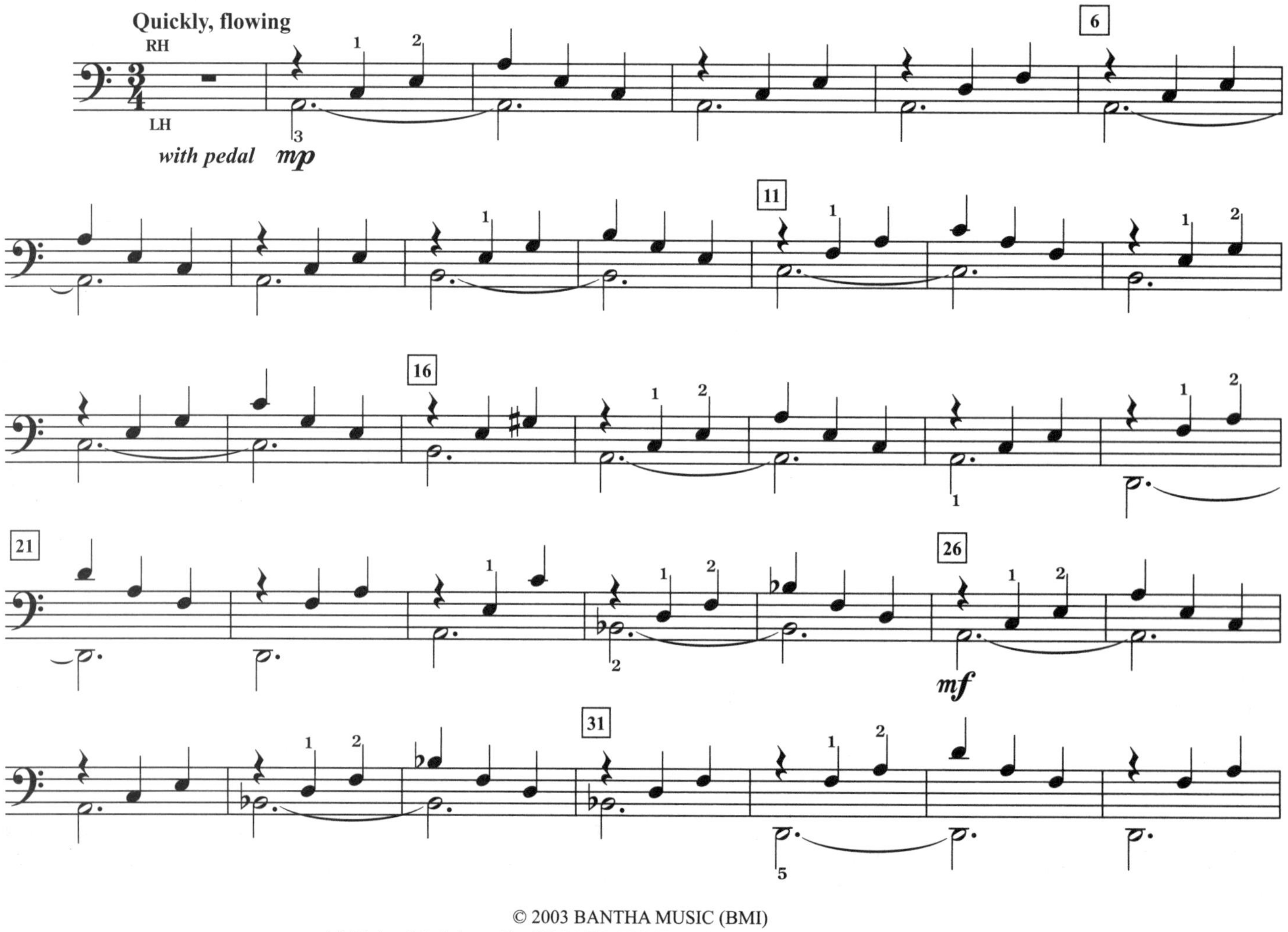

© 2003 BANTHA MUSIC (BMI)
All Rights Administered by WARNER-TAMERLANE PUBLISHING CORP. (BMI)
All Rights Reserved

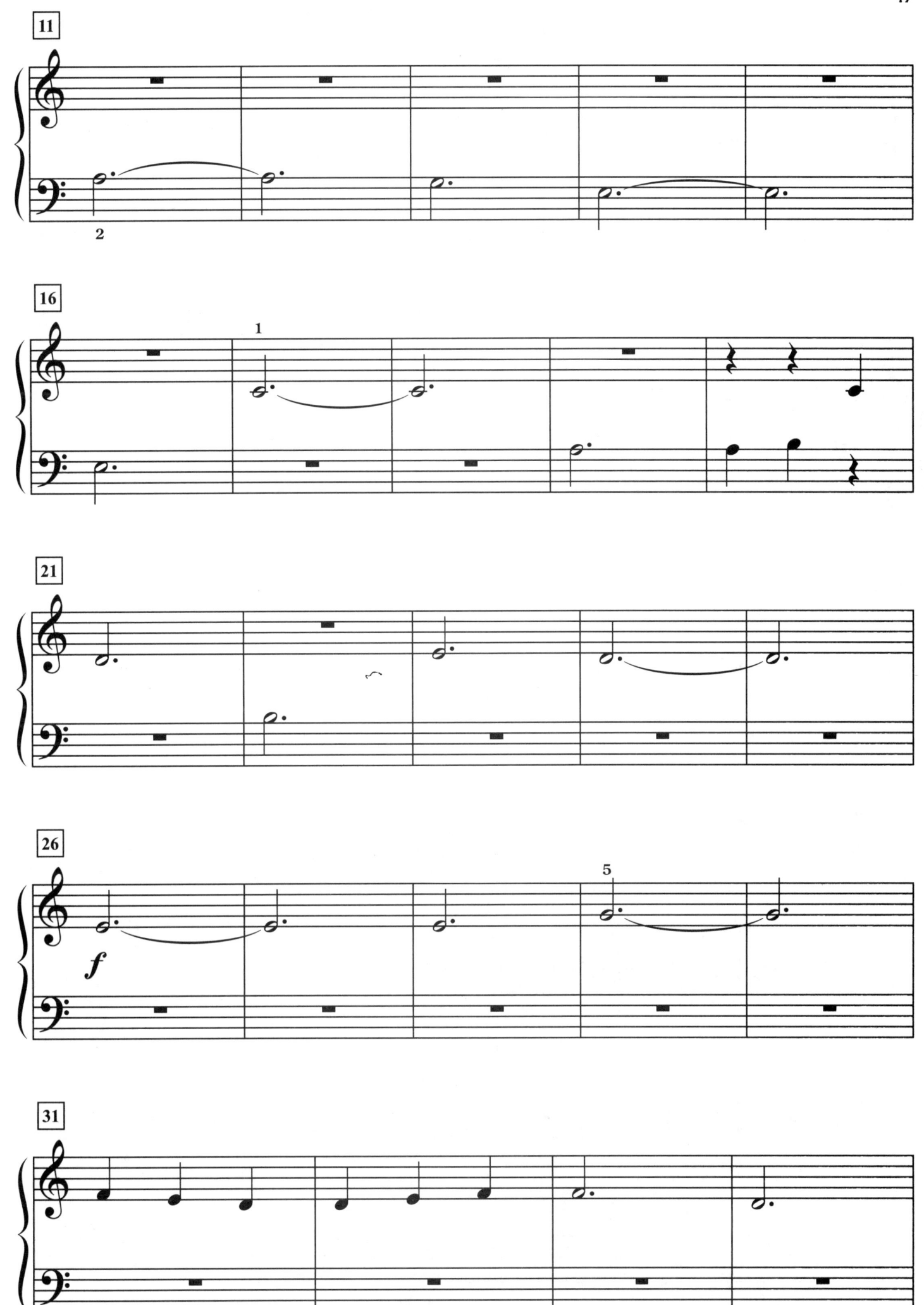

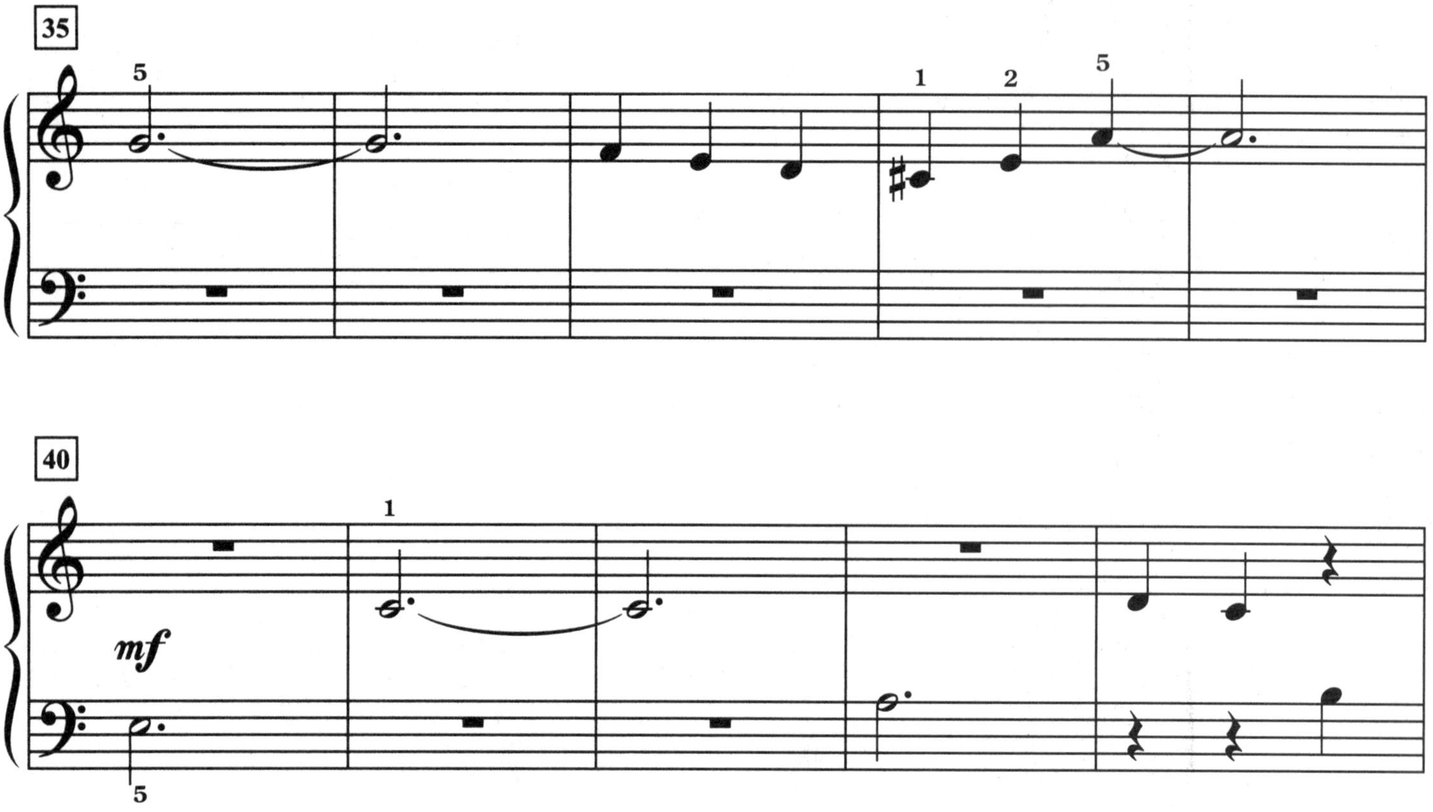

(duet continued)

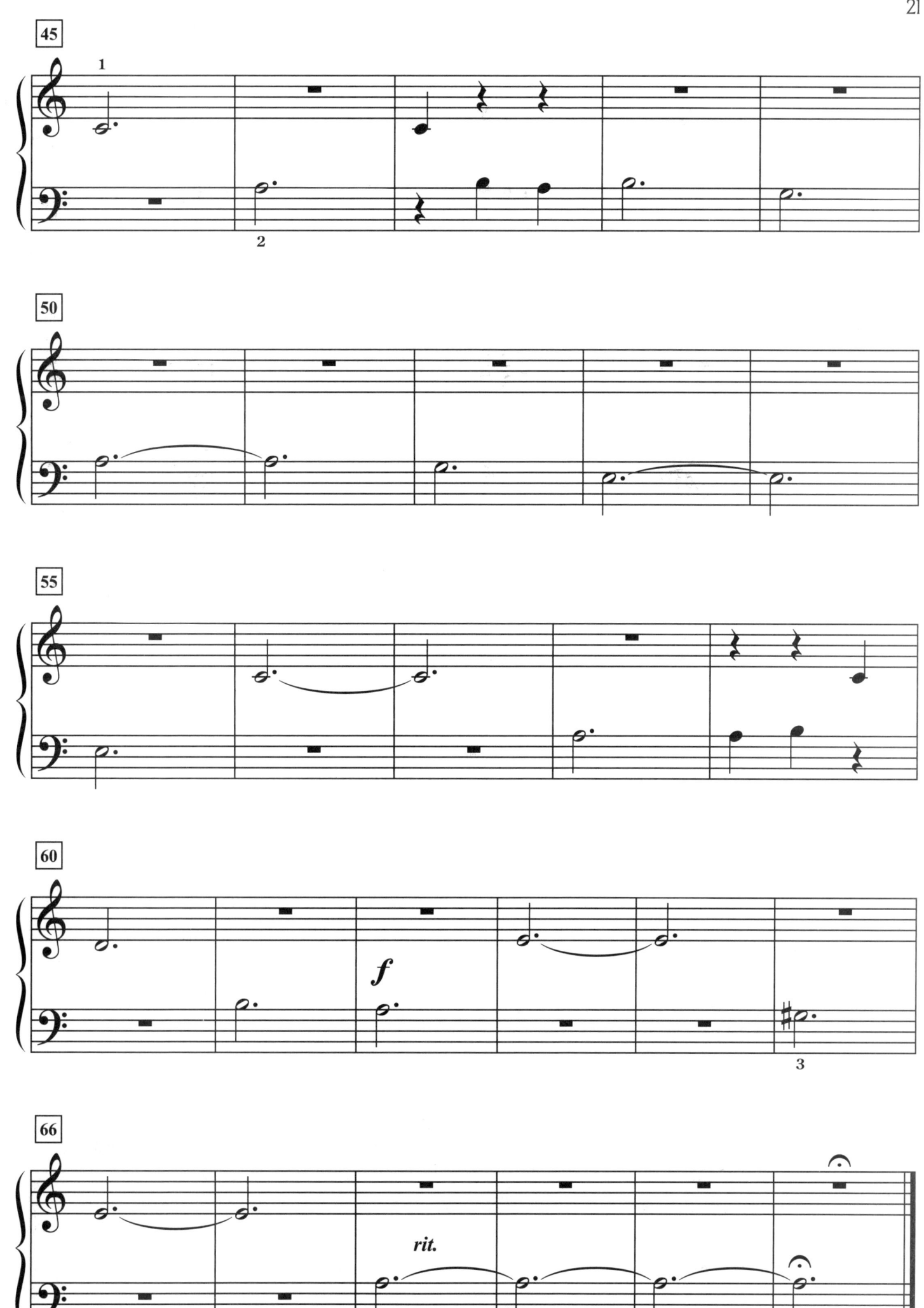

BATTLE OF THE HEROES

Music by JOHN WILLIAMS
Arranged by Tom Gerou

Optional Duet Accompaniment (Play solo part 1 octave higher than written.)

© 2005 BANTHA MUSIC
All Rights Administered by WARNER-TAMERLANE PUBLISHING CORP.
All Rights Reserved

BINARY SUNSET

Music by JOHN WILLIAMS
Arranged by Tom Gerou

Optional Duet Accompaniment (Play solo part 1 octave higher than written.)

© 1977 WARNER-TAMERLANE PUBLISHING CORP. and BANTHA MUSIC
All Rights Administered by WARNER-TAMERLANE PUBLISHING CORP.
All Rights Reserved

CANTINA BAND

Music by **JOHN WILLIAMS**
Arranged by Tom Gerou

Optional Duet Accompaniment (Play solo part 1 octave higher than written.)

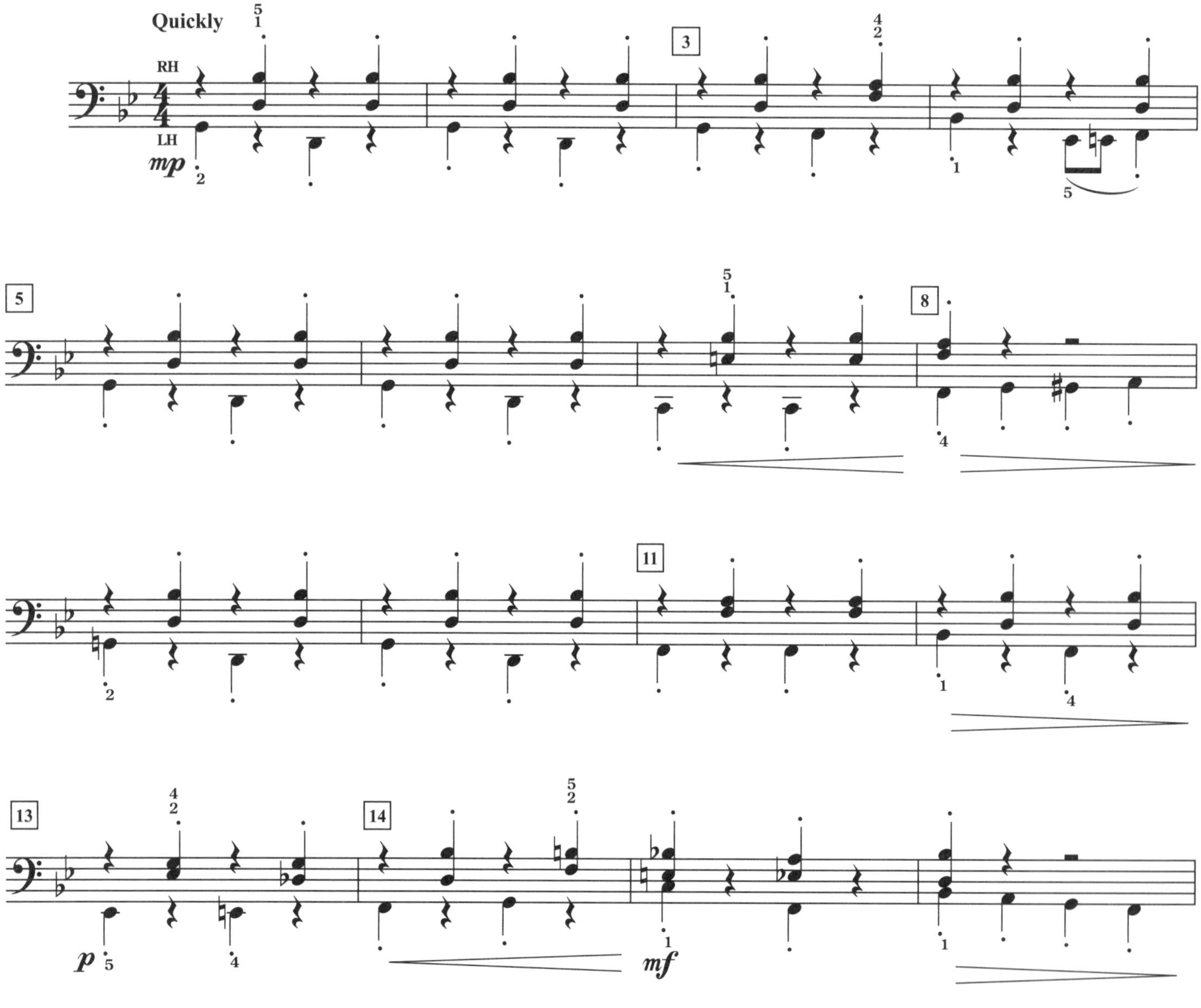

© 1977 (Renewed) WARNER-TAMERLANE PUBLISHING CORP. and BANTHA MUSIC
All rights administered by WARNER-TAMERLANE PUBLISHING CORP.
All Rights Reserved

(duet continued)

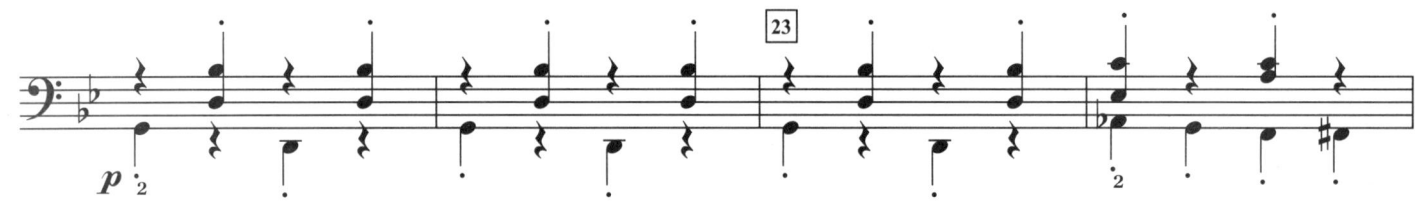

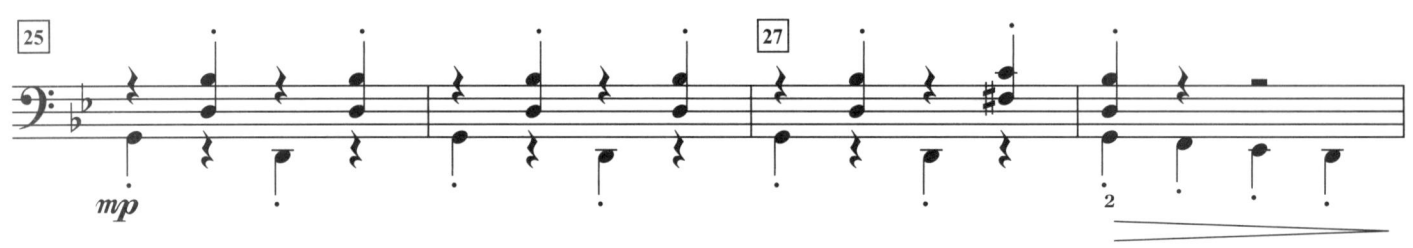

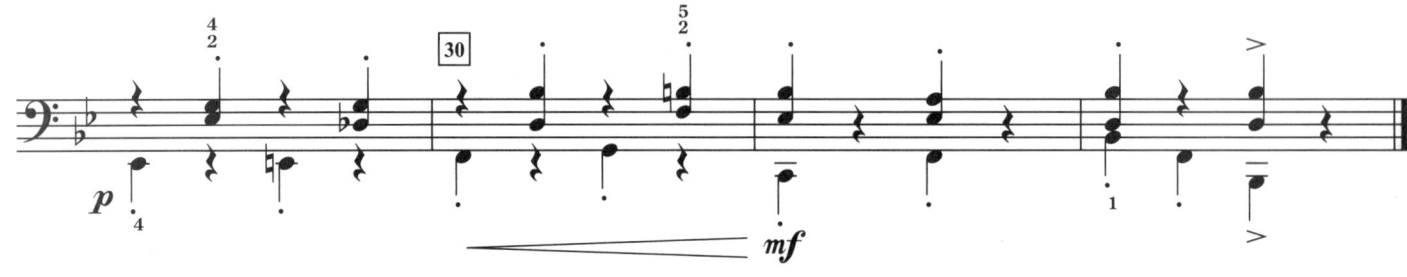

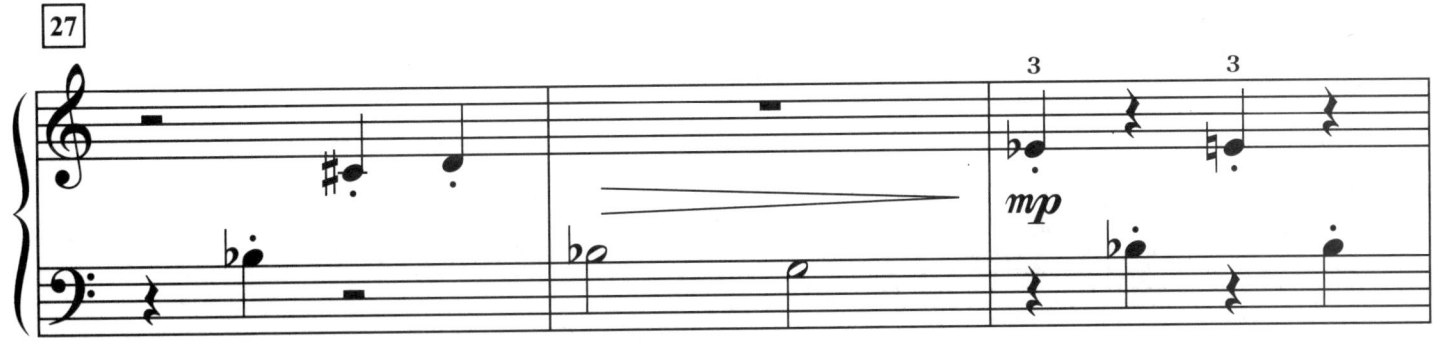

JAWA SANDCRAWLER

Music by **JOHN WILLIAMS**
Arranged by Tom Gerou

Optional Duet Accompaniment (Play solo part 1 octave higher than written.)

© 1977 WARNER-TAMERLANE PUBLISHING CORP. and BANTHA MUSIC
All Rights Administered by WARNER-TAMERLANE PUBLISHING CORP.
All Rights Reserved

PRINCESS LEIA'S THEME

Music by JOHN WILLIAMS
Arranged by Tom Gerou

Optional Duet Accompaniment (Play solo part 1 octave higher than written.)

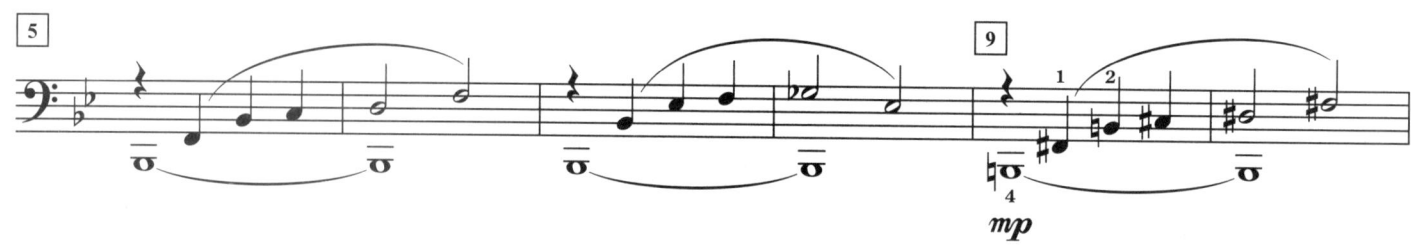

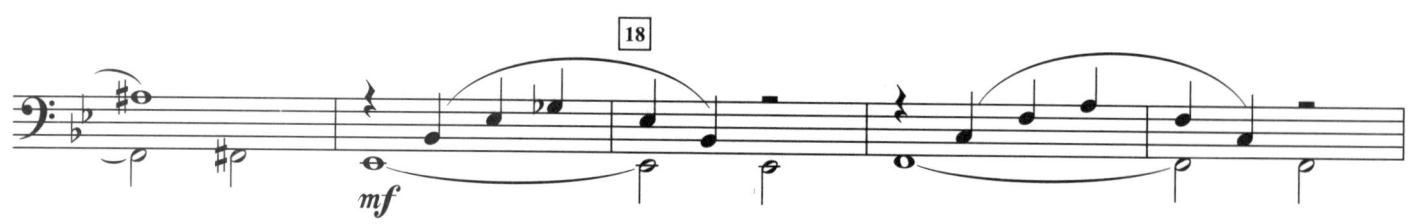

© 1977 (Renewed) WARNER-TAMERLANE PUBLISHING CORP. and BANTHA MUSIC
All Rights Administered by WARNER-TAMERLANE PUBLISHING CORP.
All Rights Reserved

34

(duet continued)

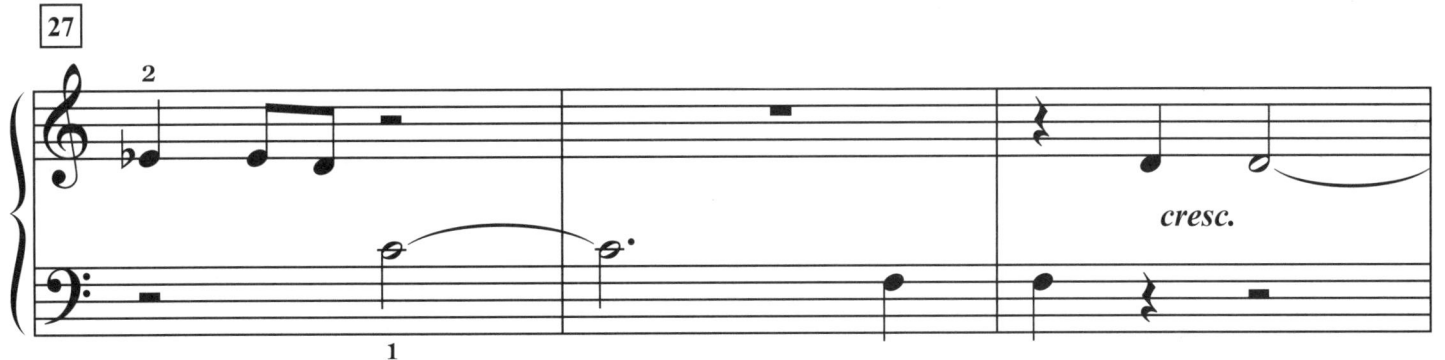

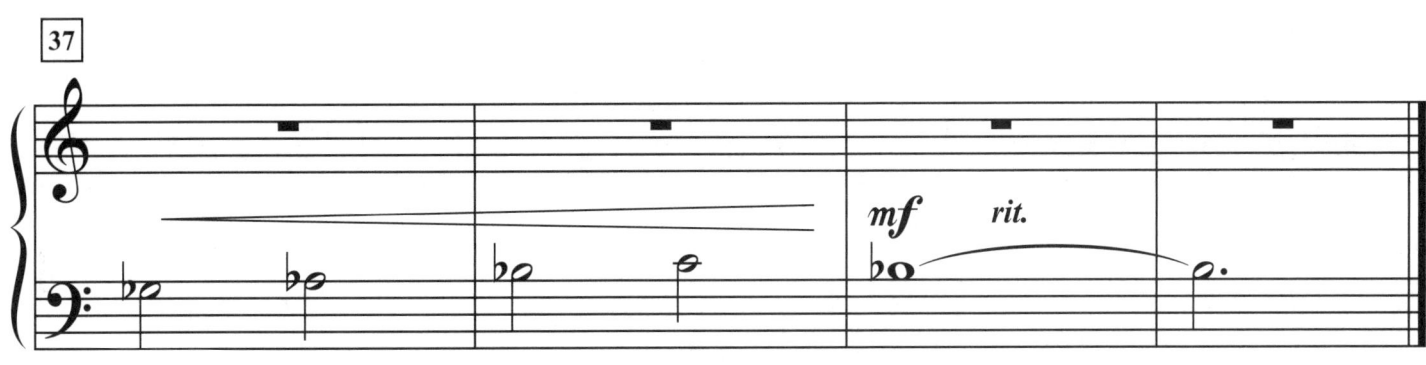

THE THRONE ROOM

Music by JOHN WILLIAMS
Arranged by Tom Gerou

Optional Duet Accompaniment (Play solo part 1 octave higher than written.)

© 1977 (Renewed) WARNER-TAMERLANE PUBLISHING CORP. (BMI) and BANTHA MUSIC (BMI)
All Rights Administered by WARNER-TAMERLANE PUBLISHING CORP.
All Rights Reserved

(duet continued)

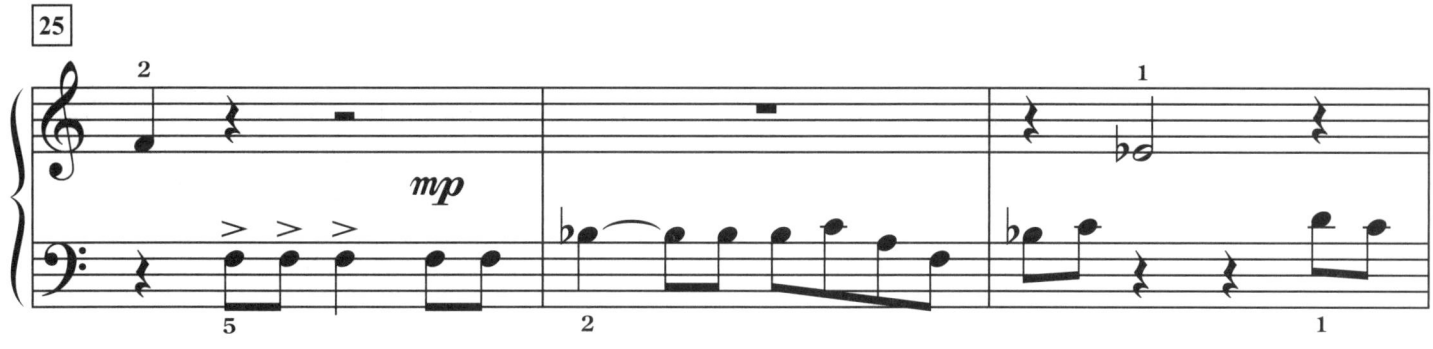
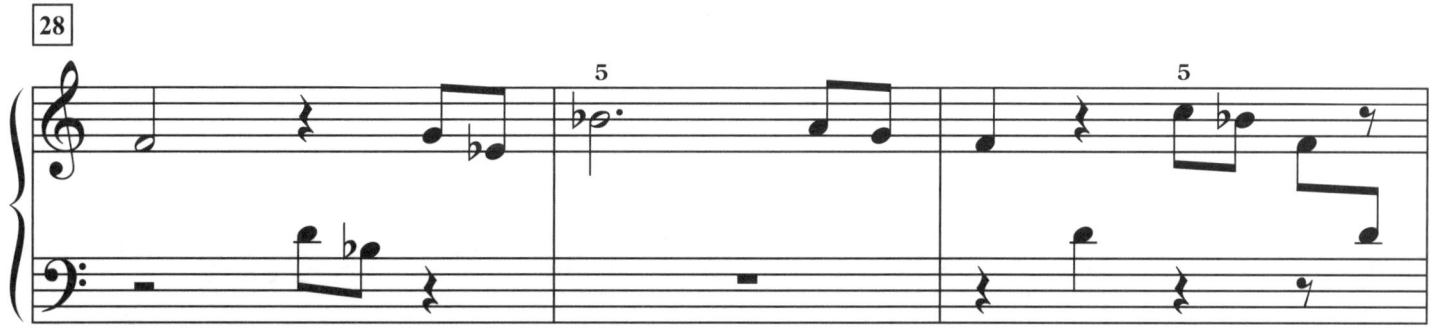
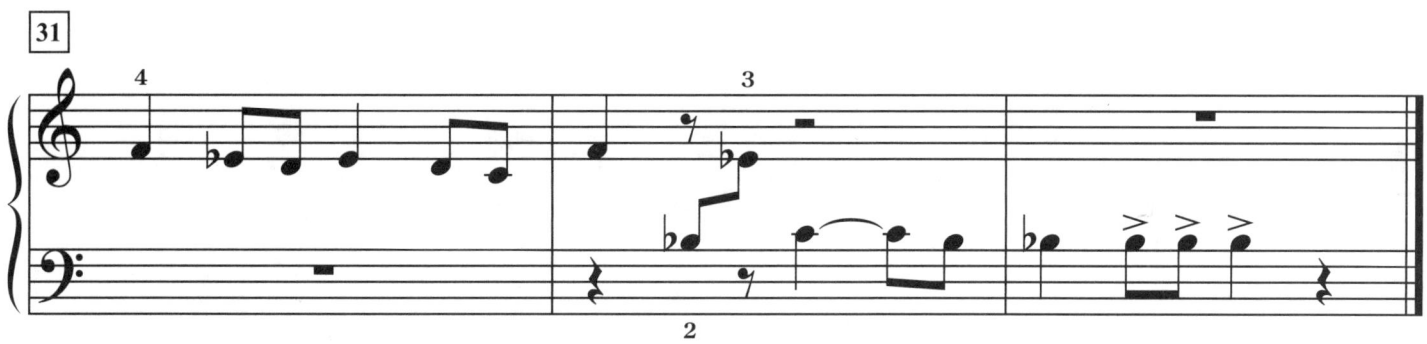

THE IMPERIAL MARCH
(Darth Vader's Theme)

Music by JOHN WILLIAMS
Arranged by Tom Gerou

Optional Duet Accompaniment (Play solo part 1 octave higher than written.)

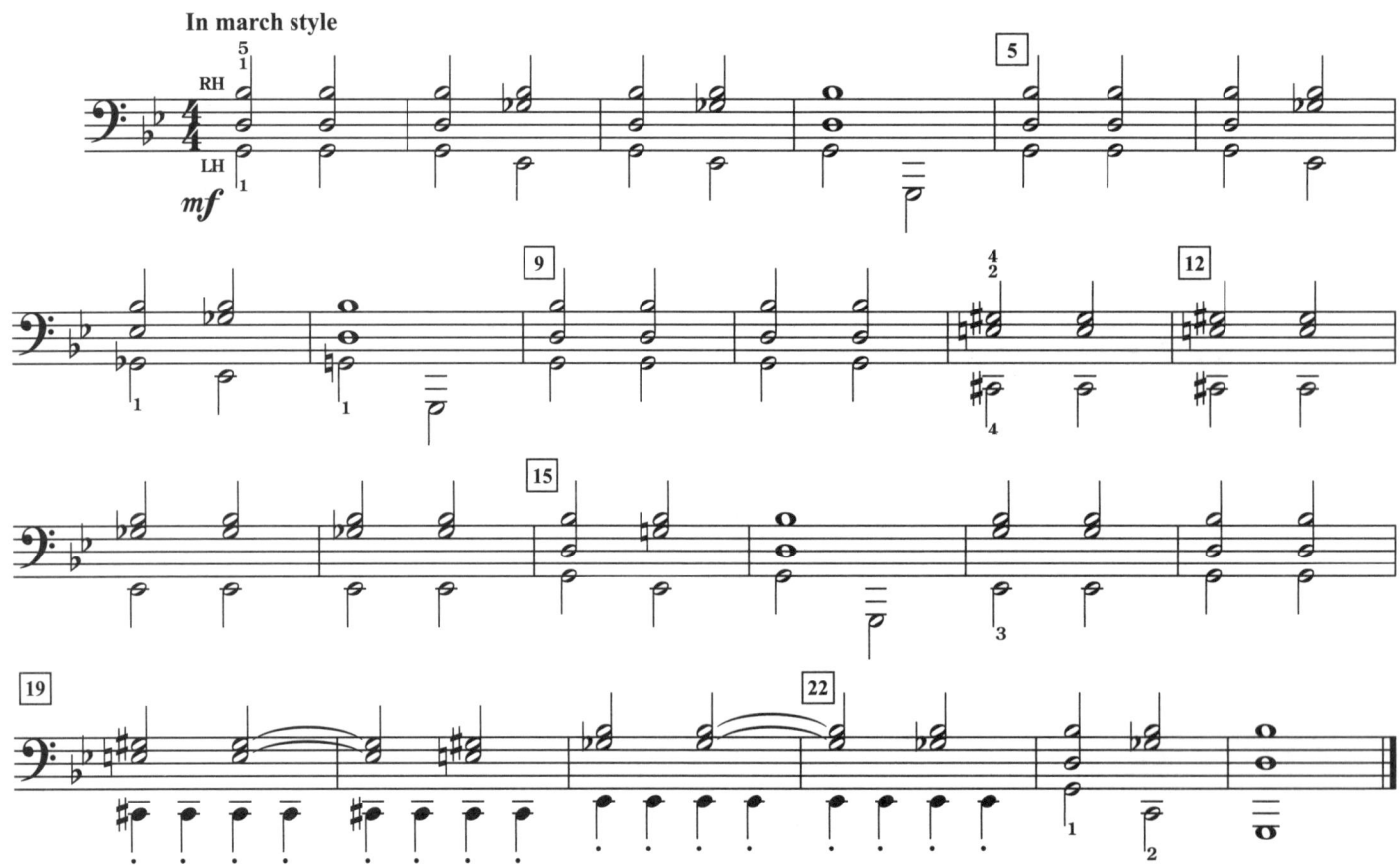

© 1980 WARNER-TAMERLANE PUBLISHING CORP. and BANTHA MUSIC
All Rights Administered by WARNER-TAMERLANE PUBLISHING CORP.
All Rights Reserved

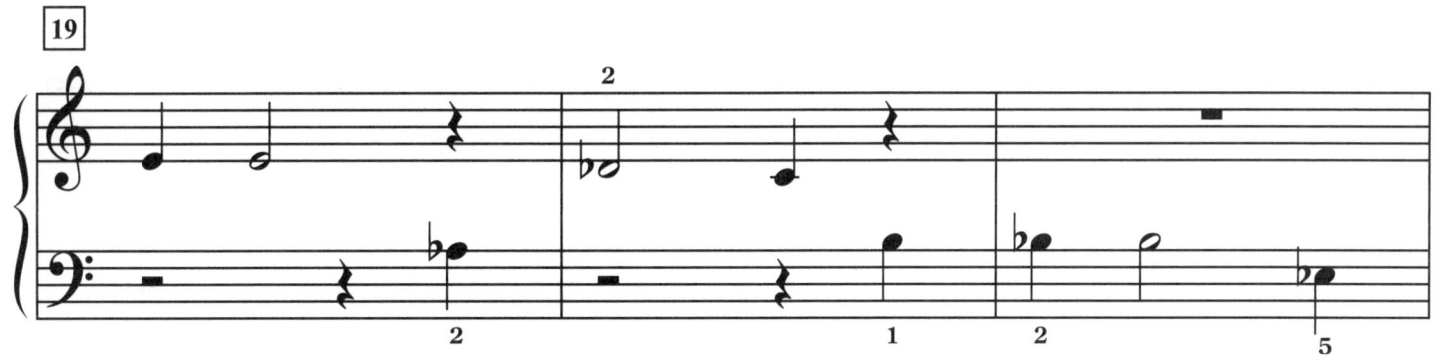

MAY THE FORCE BE WITH YOU

Music by JOHN WILLIAMS
Arranged by Tom Gerou

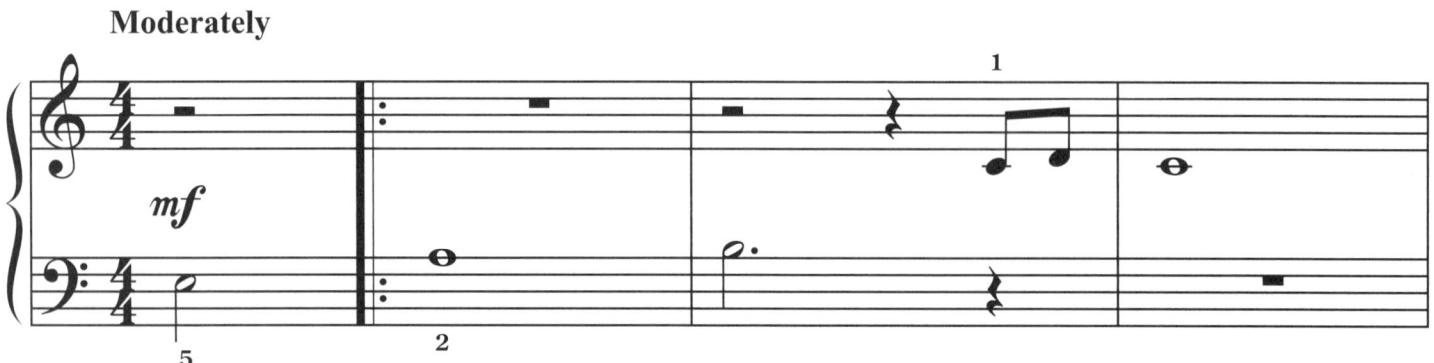

Optional Duet Accompaniment (Play solo part 1 octave higher than written.)

© 1980 WARNER-TAMERLANE PUBLISHING CORP. and BANTHA MUSIC
All Rights Administered by WARNER-TAMERLANE PUBLISHING CORP.
All Rights Reserved

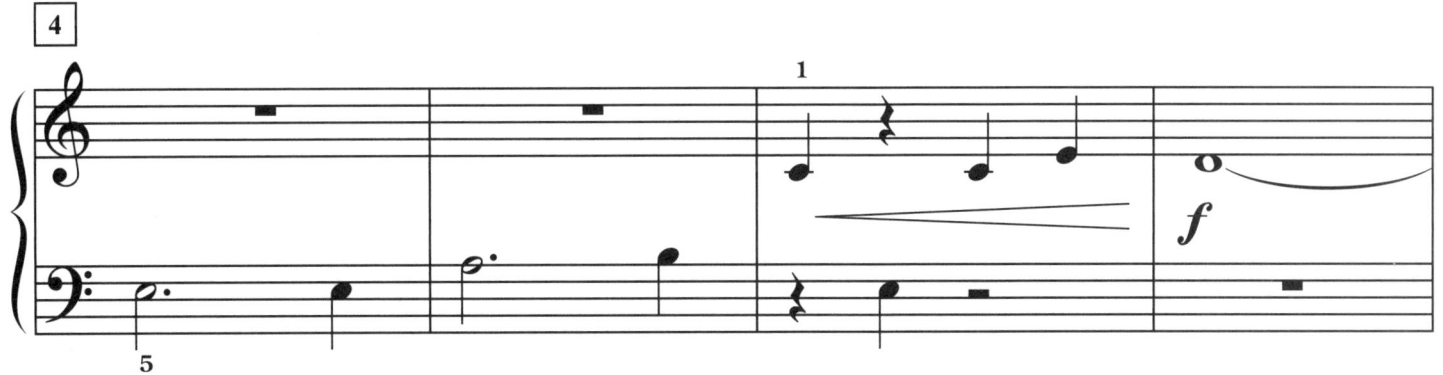

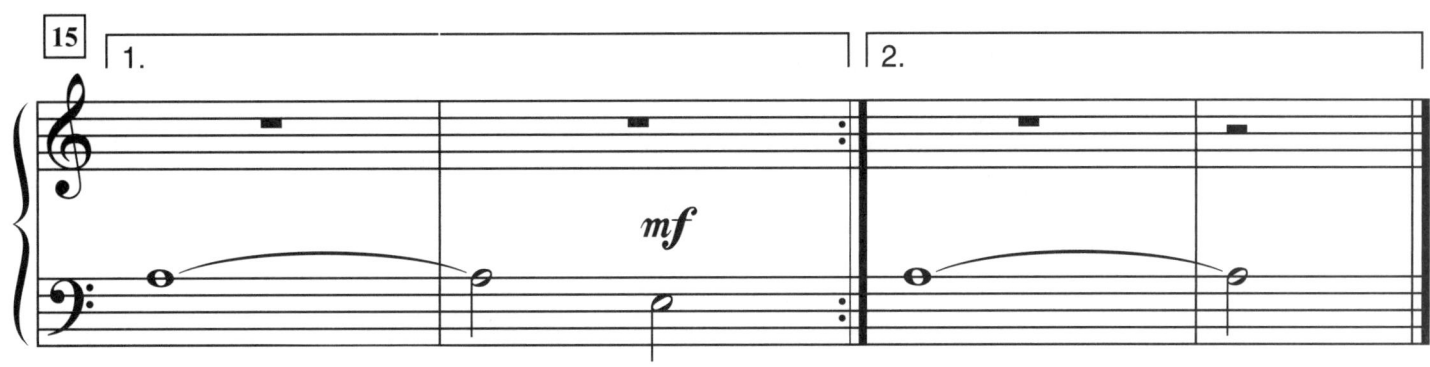

YODA'S THEME

Music by JOHN WILLIAMS
Arranged by Tom Gerou

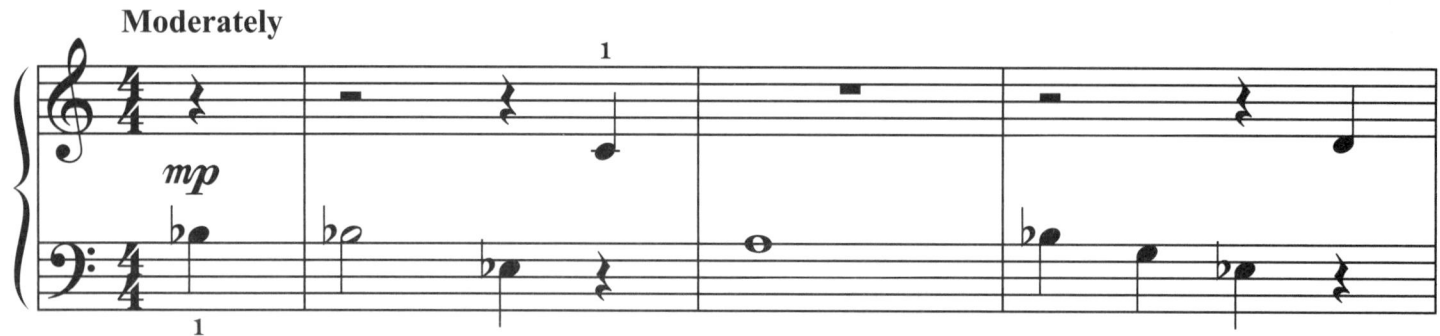

Optional Duet Accompaniment (Play solo part 1 octave higher than written.)

© 1980 WARNER-TAMERLANE PUBLISHING CORP. and BANTHA MUSIC
All Rights Administered by WARNER-TAMERLANE PUBLISHING CORP.
All Rights Reserved

(duet continued)

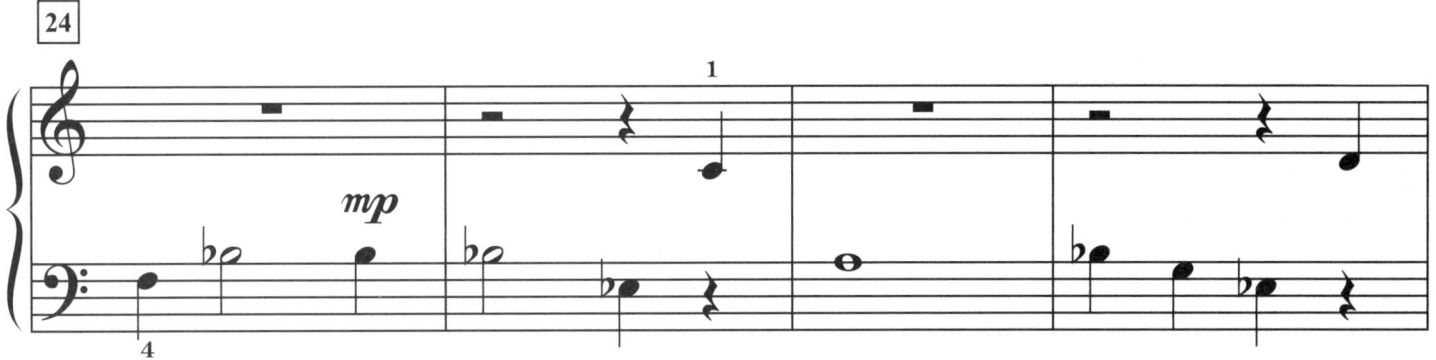

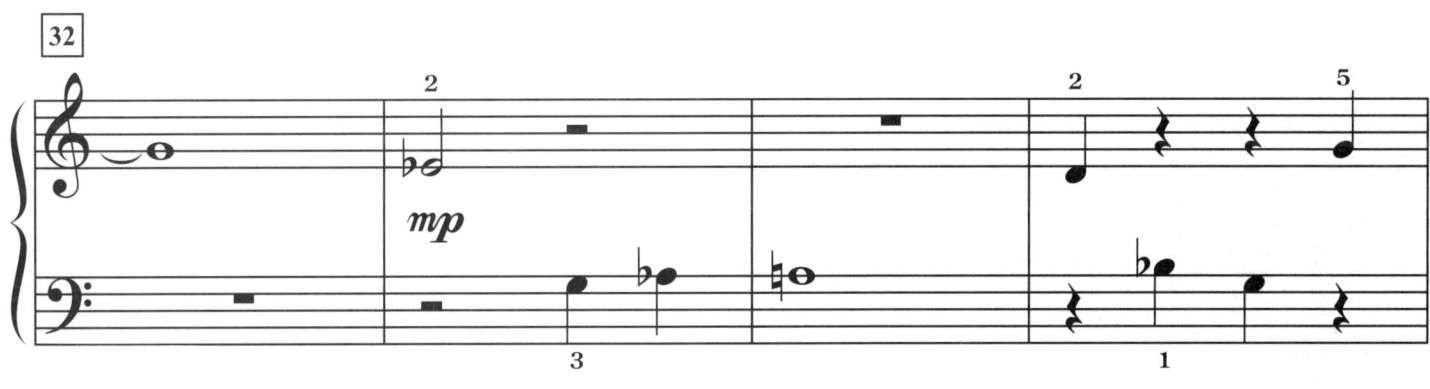

LUKE AND LEIA

Music by JOHN WILLIAMS
Arranged by Tom Gerou

Optional Duet Accompaniment (Play solo part 1 octave higher than written.)

© 1983 BANTHA MUSIC
All Rights Administered by WARNER-TAMERLANE PUBLISHING CORP.
All Rights Reserved

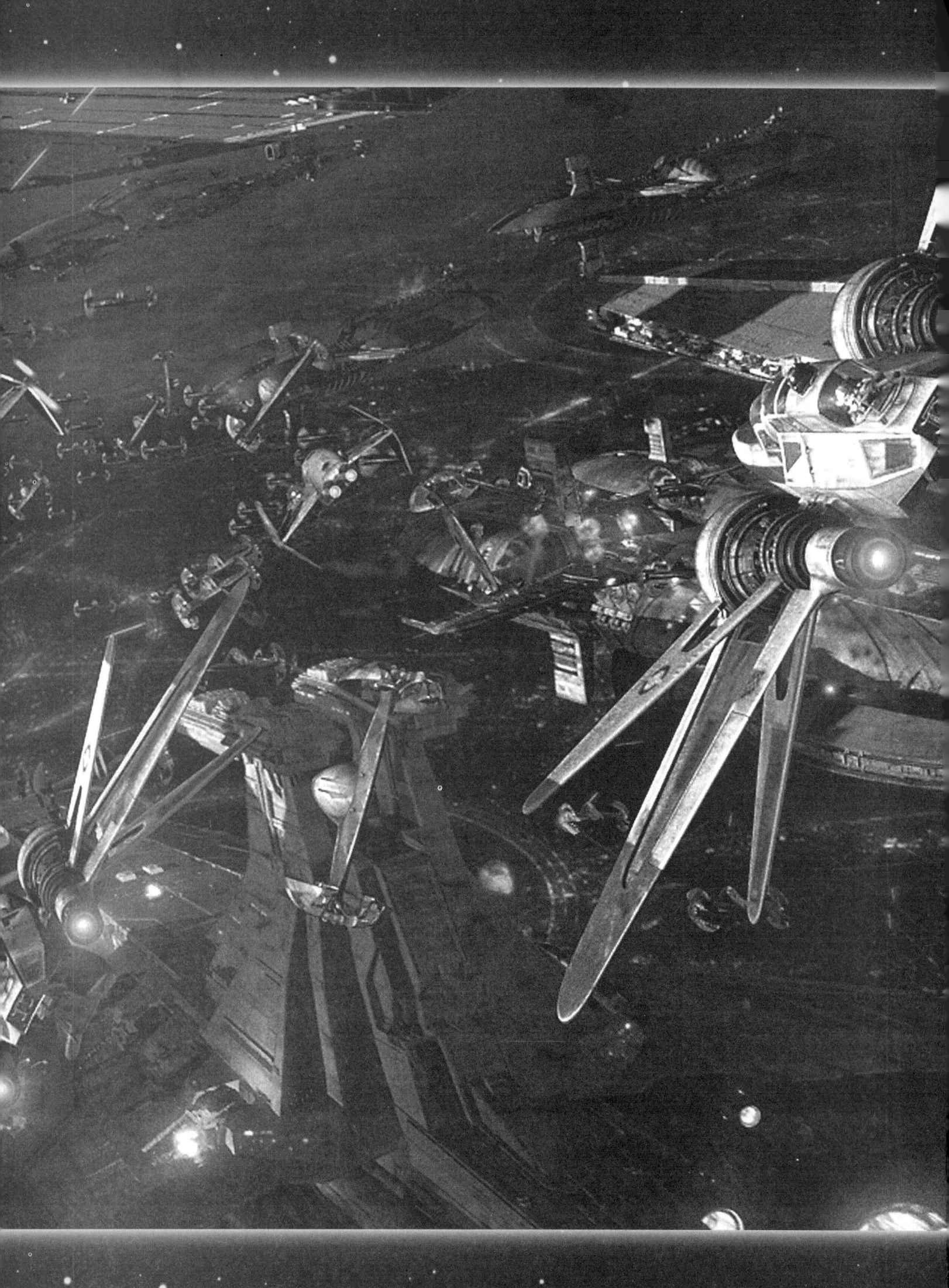